Out The Shadows

Eintou Pearl Springer

Karia Press

Out Of The Shadows

First published in 1986 by **Karia Press.**

Book Layout and Design by Buzz Johnson
Cover illustration by Sonya Walters
Cover design by Buzz Johnson

Typeset by Karia.

ISBN 0 946918 58 9 Pb

Karia Press
BCM Karia
London WC1N 3XX
United Kingdom

Printed in Great Britain by
Whitstable Litho Ltd., Whitstable, Kent

Contents

Attibon Legba	7
My Mother	9
Sunset in Santa Cruz	12
Words	15
Moon Flow	16
New Life	17
Loss	19
Abortion	21
Birth	23
Etchings	25
Temptation	27
Flying High	28
In Ting	30
Trip	32
Sans Script	35
Life Sap	36
Caribbean Man	37
Letter To A Man	38
London Blues	41
Bois	45
Twin Locks	48
Woman In Struggle	50
Release	54
Twilight Heat	56
Cloud Burst	58
Women Over 30	59
Shadows	60
On Mother's Day	63
For Single Mothers	65
On Becoming A Woman	68
Freedom Child — Tilla's Lullaby	72

K*a*l*e*i*d*o*s*c*o*p*e 74
Images 76
For Astor 79
Oil Spill 82
Blood Guilt For Maurice 85
Capital C 88
Black Balled 91
The Underground 94
White Rasta 95
Jah Say 97
Masquerade 100
Cocksure 104
Woman As Artiste I
The Leap 108
Woman As Artiste II:
Spaced 111
Woman As Artiste III:
The Workplace 115
Woman As Artiste IV:
On Walking in the Rain
To A London Bus Stop 118
Out of the Shadows 123

Dedicated to

Una Roach
Gloria Valere
Slade Hopkinson
Those who knew I would one day write
And for my mother whose sacrifices made it all possible.

Eintou Pearl Springer was born in Santa Cruz, Trinidad & Tobago, her early school education was at the San Juan Presbyterian school where she was awarded a College Exhibition to St. George's College, Barataria.

She has been involved in acting since school-days under Slade Hopkinson and joined Trinidad Theatre Workshop in 1962. There she continued working with Slade Hopkinson and other pioneering figures in Drama, Playwriting and Theatre. Later on, in 1970, she was one of the founding members of Slade Hopkinson's Caribbean Theatre Guild. After Slade was forced to leave the group due to illness, Eintou became one of its Co-Directors.

Eintou is well known for her acting. Amongst others, her roles included Mr. Rowse in CLR James' *Minty Alley* and Mavis in Errol John's *Moon on a Rainbow Shawl.* For both of these roles she received awards. She has adapted two important Caribbean Novels — CLR James *Minty Alley* (1977) and Sam Selvon's *A Brighter Sun* (November 1979). Her involvement in the dramatic arts has extended to theatre in education in Trinidad & Tobago.

Eintou is a member of the Regional Committee on Cultural Sovereighty co-ordinated by George Lamming. She is also a founder-member of the National Drama Association of Trinidad & Tobago and The Writers Union of Trinidad & Tobago and has served on the executives of both.

Eintou has performed her poetry and conducted workshops in Trinidad & Tobago and other parts of the Caribbean. In England during 1985/86, her work attracted considerable attraction and acclaim.

It is the responses to her oral presentation that has resulted in the publication of her work, of which very little has, to-date been published.

A firm advocate in women's rights, Eintou is also a qualified Librarian and is presently in charge of the West-Indian Reference Library in Trinidad, Trinidad & Tobago, The Caribbean. She is the mother of four daughters.

Attibon Legba

Attibon Legba
ouvrez bayon pour moi
Attibon Legba
ouvrez bayon pour moi.
Cry Glory, Glory to Legba!
cry praise, praise to Legba!
Elegba O
help Legba
help your children Elegba
children struggling Legba
children in turmoil Elegba
Guardian, Guardian of the roads —
the crossroads
help us —
we can't find the right road.
Master of three canals Loa O!
Attibon Legba
ouvrez bayon pour moi
Where are you
Where are you
O 'gun O —
Warrior O!
teach us again how to fight
for what is right.
Give us your spirit
your spirit of battle O'gun
Call him —
call him
Babalou O!
Houngan O!
Cadomble O!
Lucumi O!
Did you come —

did you come again
as Maurice and I killed you
Did you come
did you come again
as Walter and I killed you
Attibon Legba
ouvrez bayon pour moi
Legba O — O'gun O!
We have lost you
all of you
lost you in Jerusalem
lost you disguised in robes of white saints
Attibon Legba
ouvrez bayon pour moi
spirits moving in the trees
spirits tossing in the seas
we salute you
Walter O!
Che O!
Marley O!
Fanon O!
Butler O!
Marryshow O!
Maurice O!
Garvey O!
They have gone
Legba, Elegba
Eshu
now is me and you

They have gone
Legba, Elegba
Eshu
now is me and you.

My Mother

Roughened palms
of
pain
witness labours
of
love
for
spawnings
from
fecund
thighs.

Rivered lines
of
sorrow
testify
to
years
of
struggling
for
spawnings
from
fecund thighs.

Eyes
cold
distant
seek
to
block from

present
memory
empty
drought
filled
years
of
sacrifice
except
when
even
now
the
twisting
in
the
guts
is
prompted
by
care
for
full grown
spawnings
from
fecund
thighs

and
calloused
knees
bearing
witness
to
weary
hours
through
years
of

supplication
still
now, bend
constantly
entreating
grace
for
spawnings
from
fecund
thighs.

Sunset in Santa Cruz

Cicadas in mourning
call
across the darkening hills
lush green
pointing
to meet the
reddened yellowed
sky
and
crowning paths of
scattered huts
crowded out
making way —
for
well housed
strangers
to
damp cool
valley.
In humble huts
black sage
burning
keeps
at bay
hordes
of circling
insects.
Groves of
cocoa, citrus,
green figs
yield the
aged devotés
in call to one another —

"M'ka Allez Coucher Chez moi"
backs bent low
in weary
recognition
of
losing tongue
and skill to thrust
with tool
into the fecund dampness
beneath them.

Brash new breed
treads her
in uncaring haste,
spews only spit
into her valley
meant to
bring forth
fruit.

Tall spires
crown the
fretted arch
and generations pass
to pray
to mate
and then be
passed out
back
into the
waiting earth
to come again
as fruit.

Call of rooted navel
meeting
rotted flesh;
call of
mourning cicadas
calling the rains

fall down
down
into the
valley —
refuge for
fleeing Caribs
and
Spaniards
fleeing
the Main currents
of blood
mix with the
blood of
blacks
still fettered
in the
foetid stench
of
rotted flesh
and leaves
danced to death
beneath
the cocoa.

Rivers flowing
swiftly
slow
to
slothful pollution.
None hear
the silent screams
of she whose
maw is gutted
now
with filth.
None,
but the darkening sky.
In haste
tiny slivers
of light

flee.
Sun sets
in
Santa Cruz.

Words

Words —
a flood of
words
longing to be

Words
moving —
restless —
growing —
taking form.

Words
common labour prolonged
labour intense
short
sharp
spewed forth
alive
screaming
HOPE.

Stations (I)
Moon Flow

The angel
with the flaming sword
guards the vaults of love.
Lunar emissions
flow a sluggish path
of pain
for shredded linings.
In periodic moon flow
rich legends grow
In periodic moon flow
hope dies
or fear subsides.
For periodic moon flow
there are
emissaries —
deep depression
heightened tension
ached eruptions —
moods
labile, lacrimal
phasing fast
into moon flow
then heightened
libido
and
cyclic
regeneration.

Stations (II)
New Life
For My Daughters

Sensuous —
the feel of movement
inside me.
Sensuous —
nipples enlarging
breasts engorging
with life
supporting
fluid.

Nauseous —
The morning vomits
up the day.
Nauseous
aches and cravings,
hope overiding
the fear
the prickling
pain.

The mind peers into the womb
the mind's eyes probes the womb
in anxiety
curiousity.
No physiology can solve
the mystery
of life
encapsulated

I pat and feel and fondle
commune with life unseen
strong genes

black genes.
Fierce protectiveness
weaves plans
and dreams
for life
encapsulated

I cannot wait
to put a face
to dreams:
I cannot wait
to feel
the eager sucks
at breasts engorged
with life
supporting fluid

I cannot wait
to be fulfilled
as woman
I cannot wait
to coo and smell
hear cries
hold very close
to breasts
engorged
with life
supporting
fluid.

Stations III) Loss

Oh! it is a loss
like no other
Oh! it is a pain
no other can share.
The hope is gone
dissipated
in pools of foetid blood
and chunks of
dead tissue
that once promised
life.

No! don't just throw
it
in your bin!
No! don't handle it
like that
you in your
antiseptic white
give it a name
bury it.

I loved for that
I sweated for that
I cried out in
happiness for that
I nurtured it
inside me
on hope!

Man who shared
my love
You cannot know

my pain.
For you
my bloated belly
symbolised
only
your genes
in immortality
you cannot know
the twisting
of my guts
for that
dead lump
of tissue.

I want to drive
you — crazy!
You are
already
crazy!
You do
not understand!
I want my baby
back!
Hold me!

Stations (IV) Abortion

Do not curse me
for interrupting
your life
I did not want you.
Do not haunt me.
I did away with you!
Have I no right
to decide
what happens
inside me?

I have my guilt
for interrupting
your life.
I did not want
but to be rid
of you
Desperately!
Allow me the right
to decide
what happens
inside me!

Will God curse me
for interrupting
your life?
Will he give me
no more chances
to reproduce
life —
What do preachers
know?

Mostly —
they're men
Anyway.
They never felt
an alien
unwanted
thing —
growing
inside
them!
I did not want you!
I have the right
to decide
what happens
inside me!

Who knew my fears,
My terror.
Who felt my anguish.
I had one million
reasons
that said
you should not live!

The pangs of guilt
don't mean
that I am sorry.
I know!
I do not give life.
for me
it's just
to carry
life;
but I do have
the right
to decide
what happens
inside me.
I do —
DON'T I?

Stations (V)
Birth

Legs
distended
in tiredness.

Time suspended
in
cocoons
of
pain
and
bloody
outpourings.

Eyes
unseeing
filming
visions
of
the future
Spawned
from present
pain.

Remissions
of
pain
bringing
longing
for
comfort
and
an
end

to
Pain
Groanings
gutteral
primal
dissolve
in
high pitched
climaxes
of sound.
Shallow
uneven
breathings
push out
the
struggling mass
of eager
life
that needs
no
slap
to cry

I AM.

Stations (VI) Etchings

Memories —
etched on
aged canvas
stretched tight
on angled
bones.

Wrinkles
etched
round
empty
pain-filled
pools —
opaque windows
o-o-oh o-o-oh

Sound the sounds
of
wordless pain
for
unborn
flushed out
by caraille
and wild coffee root.
o-o-oh o-o-oh

Sound the sounds
of
wordless pain
for
loves that
could have
been

so sweet
o-o-oh o-o-oh.

Sound the sounds
of
wordless pain —
sound them
creeping upwards
now —
from flaccid guts
spreading up
to make
hands clench
and shoulders droop
o-o-oh o-o-oh

Unseeing
windows
feel the
soft warm
flesh
of
scions
breathing
hope.

Muffle
the sounds of pain
still the voice
that longs to scream
the pain
of aged wisdom.

Shared wisdom
never dulls
the urge
to feel
to know
twin parameters —
the agony

the ecstacy
etched anew
on clean firm
canvas,
o-o-oh o-o-oh
The sounds
of wordless pain
span the
generations.

Temptation

Temptation
twists
her smiling face,
lures us
with promises
of transient pleasure
ephemeral gains.
Entrapped enmeshed
within her slimy tentacles,
the face snaps
back —
revealing worms
crawling
from the putridity;
and karmic vengeance
stalks
the sated flesh
stenches the earth.

Flying High

Ode To A Beauty Queen

What you see
is what you get!
Take your time —
look and choose.
I've been on stage
for sale
a long time now.
Once it was called
an auction block,
but, well,
I'm way past that stage now.
I'm sophisticated
and dedicated
to getting
as much as I can
for what I have to give.

Don't scoff at me,
You
in the minority.
I have
National honours
on my side.
The whole nation's
on my side
I'm even flying high
in style.

I mean flesh is the "in" thing
New York's doing it,
it must be right.
I'm fed up
of the mother
wife role.

"Cutlass doh leave
no mark in water;"
but babies,
uh uh,
that will scar
and mar
the goods.
Look at me
you sweet young things
Come fly with me
I'm flying high.
Chuck the books —
career.
Books are good
for those
who don't have
the goods.
Flesh is
the easiest way to national honours
and flying high.

I'm sure you want
to be just like me —
hair all straightened and nice
face all painted and bright —
and the flesh
ooh the flesh,
lovely gorgeous hunks of it —
pouring out
of skin tight tights
and decolletage.
Let me influence you,
blow your mind.
Come fly with me —
I'm flying high
come fly with me —
I'm flying high.

In Ting

Lesbianism
is de in ting
You in?
me eh in!

Homosexuality
is de in ting
You in?
me eh in!

Ambidexterity
is de in ting
You in?
me eh in!

Breaking up
is de in ting
Is breaking up
breaking out
Or breaking in
You in?
me eh in!

Cocaine ah hear
is de in ting
You in?
me eh in:

Ah hear dey say
dat man say
Woman dread.

Ah hear dey say
dat woman say
Man pushing
a wicked head

So man for man
and woman for woman
So dey say
I wasn't dey!

To flaunt deviance
as societal defiance
Don't give answers
Is just postures
empty gestures
If you do it
then that's your trip
Keep it private
I may think it's sick.

Dey eh happy!
is only gallery.
Is ah emptiness
belief in nothingness.
We must realise
is time to internalise —
find we spirit self
commit we self
to self respect.
Changes to make
A new road to take

Lesbianism
is de in ting
You in?
me eh in!

Trip
(for Beverly Jones)

The glitter of disco lights
beckon,
they entice
they hypnotize.
Come young people
come
find release from
the frustration
the harshness
the reality

Trip
young sister
parade your flesh
for pennies
pennies
in the beauty market

Trip
freak out
blow your mind
take a drug
and another
and another
and find
an ease
to worries
problems

Drugs
the lights

the bright lights
Toronto for Divali
New York for Labour Day.
Leave home
for the holidays
trendy clothes
from Miami
end of summer
sales.

Trip
join the Jesus freaks.
Flash
your symbols,
crash your identity.
Hide it
under veils
and male
prerogative.

Trip-dread!
Get into ideology.
All the isms.
Run some gun —
talk.
Trip
you would-be freedom
fighters,
trip into banditry.
Let your elders
who know better
invite you
to senseless slaughter
provide more Beverlys
for wasteful martyrdom,
send you ill prepared
for Babylon's guns,

Trip
wallow in the depths
depravity
one night stands
lesbianism
another sister's husband —
all the trips
that proclaim you oh
so hip:
For you are so young
afraid
resentful
of the world of your mothers
you fall so willingly
easy prey to
adventure
voyages into the unknown.

Would you believe there's nothing new:
The trip is a trap:
It's the same old shit:
The double standards
double exploitation
the man
the society
the daughters become the mothers
the beat goes on . . . .

Sans Script

Lines unscripted
unrehearsed
Actress
Naked
feeling for
words.
No remembered lines
Simply
I love you.

Eyes unconvinced —
probing
mine
hoping they're
true
the unscripted lines
I love you.

Exposed emotions
Hoping
Sparks
of response fly
from
The unscripted line
I love you.

Life Sap

Give me of the sap of
life
and I shall come
alive
again
as Woman.

Share with me
male energy
complete me —
for so it is
ordained
from always

Caribbean Man

Prolonged infant
suckled
in matriarchal relays
twixt breasts
of stifling fondness.
Growth to manhood
stunted
in perennial milk.
The cock let go
spews the sperm
scattered
over wide expanse
of irresponsibility,
makes
a new generation
of breasts
atrophy;
and tears fall
as milk flows
for infants
needing paternity,
for manchild
suckled
in matriarchal relays
twixt breasts
of stifling fondness

Letter To A Man

I can no longer
remain unfulfilled
in so many
facets
of my being.

Even our lovemaking,
before
it transported me
to ecstacy.
Now
it palls
disgusts,
it's so empty.
I love you
but no longer
will I be
sacrificed
on the altar
of your ego.

I know not
what else
to give you
or how else
to say
I love you.

I have given
pleasure and
in the pleasure
children.

I have
with pleasure,
fed your body
and tried
to feed your soul.
But I must
as well
fulfill
my own being.

Why do you hate my strength?
I seek not
my love
to compete with you,
but to reach the heights
of my own being
as you strive to reach
the heights of yours.

You claim, with words
respect for woman,
but still you hold
the concept
of the deputy.

You seek
the creation of change,
but still you revel
in the decadence
of the now.

I am repelled
when your mouth
finds mine
and the liquor
on your breath
is all I smell.
I am repelled
when you refuse

the rearrangement of
of responsibilities
that your times
demand.
To work
and care your child
is not, my love
to be less man
but simply
to extend
the sharing.

I need your understanding.
I too have needs
I too must battle
with the problems
with hassles
and need your comfort!
Are you not scared,
my love,
by the break down
of black relationships
everywhere.
Will you never learn
the one word
that can save us —
compromise

For we now understand
no longer
can afford
to blame our history;
we who understand
must learn
now
for our children
now for our society
now for ourselves —
learn
to move —
together.

London Blues

Yeow!
Is you!
Yes is you I calling!
Like you doh know me
in dis town!
Like you doh recognise
is me
What bearing wid you
and bearing you
on mih back
in mih belly
for 500 years.
Is you ah calling!
You — you!
Look you!
You walking in dis town
You eye blank —
What happen —
I doh look like woman —
ah doh feel —
like woman.

Goat bite me
crapaud pee on me
or is razor blade
ah have
between these legs!

I say
you liberate
I say
dat plenty water
pass

under de bridge
that did damn we
in a feeling
of black inferiority.
But ah get
ah shock!
Political man
artistic man
liberated man
all still running down
the white woman
in dis town!

Dem an all
ha to tell ME
they shock
how black man
fighting
to get under
dey frock.

eh you!
Smile wid me
nuh!
is you
Hold me nuh.

Is you
who churren mudder
like me,
who have a mudder like me,
and who ready
to disown me
for sleeping wid who
you call
the enemy,
like you prefer me
to make Zami.

Ah can't live widout
male company

Goat eh bite me
crapaud eh pee on me
and is not razor blade
between dese legs!

you forget
is me
you does come by
when you can't get
nutten else.
Even in the Caribbean
you tief mih head
you telling me
if you eh red
you dead;
and is not politics
you talking
So what you really saying

Well!
In London town
In all dem big city
Is here you could live out
all you fantasy
I five hundred years
I dreaming
and yearning.
Big man like you boasting
bout when you see me
wid mih white ting!
I wouldn't really mind
if was for sincere loving
But is only the historical
breaking
of that taboo
that you seeking —

and like goat bite me
and crapaud pee on me.

You keep on walking!
You ha the feeling
that when you ready
to come home
You go find me waiting.
Brother, in these times
that is a chance
you taking —
because
goat eh bite me
crapaud eh pee
on me
and is not razor blade
I have
between these legs

And de water running low
in de well ah understanding
Man — history keep repeating
while you dey
pussy chasing
you keeping the revolution
waiting
because
goat eh bite me
crapaud eh pee on me
and is not razor blade
I have
between these legs
and de water running low
in de well ah
understanding

Bois
For Leroy Clarke

There are no men!
The cult of warrior-hood
has died —
almost.
There are no men
the sheathed bois
rises only
to engage in combat
in the belly of woman!
slakes and sates
in moist effusions
that are not blood.
Are there really no men!

I want there to be
some
one
just one for me!
who will not look at me
and strip me
with his eyes
imagine how it is
between my thighs.
There are no men.

Are there really no men
who are more strong
than I,
with whom I can share —
everything,
give respect
without bondage?
No — there are no men.

Are there really no men
responsible and caring
gentle but strong
as rock unmoving?
There are no men.

Do you think
I want to be
man and woman
mother and father
protector and provider
It is because
there are no men
to whom I can
with joy
entrust myself
for guidance
share thoughts
and words
and silence.

Are there really no men?
I'm tired of coping alone
My forehead
weary now
longs to kiss a
shoulder in submission
sometimes —
but
there are no men.

And so
the ache of want
becomes a high
of celibacy
transcended to creativity
because
there are no men
worthy even

to climb
on my belly.
Are there really no men?

IF
there's such a man
answer me
quickly.
Take from me
willing submission
without violence or
suppression.
Receive as prize
for re-established
warriorhood
the moistness
for your bois
between my thighs.

Twin Locks
London '83

A French tongue
moves
in my head.
Moves slow —
teasing;
moves strong —
demanding;
twists feelings
sans help
from
French words.
Hands of warrior exile
speak
of feelings
that need
no alien
tongue to help
articulation.
And I,
feel
the moistness of response.
Locks
shade
the loveliness of
jet black
face.
Locks
his and
mine,
draw
near —
linking

black
diaspora;
and I,
feeling
the growing urgings
of maleness
know —
that
I
must
run,
or else,
move
to fuse,
our
blackness
in surrender.

Woman In Struggle

Don't ask me if I love you!
I will not conceive of it.
I will not admit to it.
I won't deal with it!
It is not true that I want you.
Do not believe the tautness,
the wetness,
The tremors in my frame.
They are just the urgings
of weak flesh
that must be mortified.
Do not notice them
Ignore them!
Don't let them make you bolder.
You must be crazy.
I can take it
and sublimate it!

Don't ask me if I trust you
How can I know it?
It's hard to test it.
Perhaps years of devotion
will end if there's possession,
acceptance
of less than substance!
What can you give me?
What if you use me
for extra duty?
Sex not clear like ideology
it messy, messy!

I need to like myself
to keep my self-respect.
Please understand it —
I fear to start it
and then can't end it.

Don't tell me that I'm cruel
I don't accept it —
I don't want to do it.
The ache you sense
is not the pain of want
but sadness at your off'ring.
I want to stay so,
I am a woman black!
Ripe!
Fertile but fallow,
beauty, creativity!
It's not that I am selfish
give me completeness,
for me that's justice
I want everything!
I crave it
and I deserve it.

Don't ask me if I'm burning.
You cannot quench me.
You cannot fill me.
I don't need this!
A little something sometimes
won't do for searing passion.
I want the first position!
I demand it!
Totality!
Be first and only.
You don't want less!
Then will I release to you
the fullness of my being —
Then will I allow

the flames
of eyes . . . .
of hands . . . .
of tongue . . . .
Till then, don't try it!
I will not buy it!

Don't tell me it is righteous.
It is not that!
It can't be that!
You can't be serious.
We search for truth,
a society that's just;
we must
reach beyond our needs, wants!
How we live is important
to make others conscious.

Don't let me know shame
It is not worth it
Why don't you listen
Have you no reason
Are you in season!
My mind's against it
Don't make me do it.

Don't ask me to live falsehood
I have my values
I have a conscience
Don't make me doubtful.
Please will you stop it!
Your bed of duty calls
I won't allow this!
I will resist it!
Even while I wilt
with want
I won't
by sheer force of will
except
this once,

this once,
for now
for memories,
for always.
I cannot fight it
God, I can't fight it.

Release

Let the dam burst.
For too long
the waters of love
have sought
and been blocked
from release
to easing
flow.

Let the dam burst
Since you would will it.
Be careful though
that you
who would dare
turn water on
be not drown-ded
in tide
longing
to
flow.

Let the dam burst.
I want to see
if you stand
poised
on one foot
set to run
wanting
only
to start the flood
but not
to join
the flow.

The dam
has long been
locked
against all
comers
until
your urgent key
tinkling tickling
at the bar-red
gates
at last
have teased
the flood gates
open
wide.

And the water
breaks
loose
As the dam
bursts
sweeping aside
the barriers
that can
not now
stop the flow.

Let the dam burst
Let the water flow
Let the dam burst
Let the water flow
and let me
be satisfied.

Twilight Heat

My breasts are very soft
cup them
in your hands —
gently now.

Remember them there
longing
to be petted
and kneaded
until
a tiny mound of
black
stands firm
on
soft base of
yellow carib root.

My eyes are full of love.
Sink yours
deep in them
until the fire
in mine own
reflect in
yours.
Let them
meet mine —
boldly
now

My hair is strong,
wiry
braided carriers of current

to your hands
from
every heated outlet
of my being.
Touch these wires
only
if you dare
brave the sparks
of response.
Touch them
now

Stop being so cerebral.
Even you —
need symbiosis
that is not mental.
Now
in the warm light,
of almost night
I feel a yearning
a restlessness.
It augurs ill for you
who would be shy,
and think
I sense not
what you try
to hide
neath words
and covert looks.

Take me down, love
from cold
pedestal of ebony
if that would mean
you fear to touch
to taste.
let me desert
my roles
of coper
wife and mother

and more
and more.
I want to
chuck them
all
and just be lover.

Cloud Burst
London '83

Thoughts of you
are
a warm oasis
in this cold;
able to thaw
all of me,
into damp heat
When I come
home
and your cloud
of warmth
bursts
all over me.

Women Over 30

Ripe —
in season
full blown
excellence.
No more half ripe
force ripe
fruit changed from green-ness
achieving fullness
of taste
of smell.

Ripe
in season
full ripened
excellence,
not for just any harvest
but for
cherished handling
mature sav'ring
of taste
of smell.

Ripe
knowing worth
enough
to refuse
to choose
who picks the fruit
who is allowed the fruit
at point of greatest
succulence.

Shadows

I sit and watch the day
dying
in final
blood red splashes
of defiance,
threatening
to come again
defeat
the all prevading darkness
poised
in conquest.

I sit and watch the sea
wild —
untramelled
like our passion
billowing still
beneath the darkness
not now seen
but heard
felt
waiting
for the light of day.
It comes for the sea
It does not come
for you
for me

You offer me
a love
in shadow;
A love
passionate

but unseen
raging —
but invisible
like the sea in night time.

What I feel for you
transcends
the raging passions,
defies
distorting shadows,
is pure enough
for mountain tops
visible
to all the world;
is warm
like sun on water
in the heat of day.

You've probed
my raging waters
You know
my tranquil depths.
Not for me
the foul and
murky waters,
not for me
the shadows.

I let you go
into the night
of shallow stagnant pools,
I shut out
the memories
and feel
the empty ache
of lonely night —
more welcome though
than shadowed
murky love

Darkness
swallows up
our love.
I watch you go
still the passions rage
tossing in restlessness
never
knowing stillness.
I watch you go.

The salt sprays
my face;
puny drops
for par-ched desert
I fear the fertile waters
of a love
spawning fruit
doomed
but to die.
I watch you go
shut out the memories.
I feel the empty ache
of lonely
night.

On Mother's Day

WOMAN — MOTHER
you whose womb
throbs
with urgent, pulsing life —
look around you —
hang your heads
in shame.
For from your bellies
have been spewed
the varied distortions
of humanity
that people the earth.

Something is wrong
very wrong.
What we see around us
is an indictment
so terrible
we would think
our wombs accursed.

WOMAN — FIRST TEACHER
what did you teach your child?
What did you not
teach your child?
How have you moved
to protect him
from the currents of doom
swirling around him
waiting eagerly
to swallow him up.

Why do your sons
insult and exploit
womankind?
Is it the influence
of that first woman
they knew?

Why, women,
do your daughters walk
with heads bowed
in ignorance
of their worth?
Come now,
they will judge you harshly,
your children,
and
as they mouth
the meaningless platitudes
on "Mothers' Day"
and wallow
in a shallow
commercialised
sentimentality

Does the knowledge
of the truth
of you — mother
mock their words?
Does the testimony
of their lifestyles
do you proud —
mother — teacher —
first teacher.

For Single Mothers

I watch my children sleep.
   Now
the fear can show.
   Now
the aches and pains
take centre stage.
   Now
swamping me
the ache for comfort
to fight
shadows —
imagined
spectres
echoing
reality.

I watch my children sleep
and love swells.
My fingers trace
blessings
on unlined foreheads
Stilled now —
small voices
crying out
their million varied needs.
Still in sleep,
the rivalries persist.
Fledgling egoes —
push elbows out
to claim
their space
I watch them sleep.

still —
at last
from endless ministrations
the fear
can show.

Not always
is there joy
in service;
not always
do the tender feelings
flow.
Often comes
the silent screaming
to flee far
from
clinging stifling
responsibility.
Often
the terror
of wrong directions
wrong decisions
made alone
with hope
with desperate prayers.

I watch my children sleep
and suddenly
a knowledge —
a new terror
new fears;
for growing up
is going away,
taking away
the distraction
of
endless ministrations,
facing
a new aloneness.

I watch my children asleep
and take refuge
in desperate prayers.
They must never know.
The fear
must never show.

On Becoming A Woman

for my first born Denise

Watching you grow
to womanhood
seeing you
venturing into life,
questing —
hoping —
brings back
memories;
memories
of the pain
the love,
that bore you,
makes the pain
swell again;
reminds me
of that first pain
signalling
Birth.

Your birth.
A pain
so sharp
so intense —
in fear
in terror
I cried out
stood on my head
held tight . . . .
to my own mother
bathed in tears;
wanting to take
my pain

as hers
knowing she could not.

And if my love
could cushion you,
then never
would you know
the pain
of being
WOMAN.
Never
would you know
the pain
of hurt
rejection
betrayal
as I.

And if my love
could protect you
from all
who would come near
and then hurt you,
then life for you
would be
the happiness
that flooded me
when first
I held you

My baby —
you were
so beautiful.
You are —
so beautiful.
Flesh of my flesh
mirror
of my dreams,
like my mother

could not
shield me
Alas!
My love —
and hers
cannot shield you
from pain
cannot hold back
the march
of years —
Inexorable.

And so —
I feel the pain
again;
that pain
heralding
your eagerness
to be born
Again —
I fell that quickening
inside me
that said
you lived
you moved.

First child
child
of my first love
no longer
coocooned
in my womb
I cannot
protect you
from the pain
of being
WOMAN.

BUT
I can
with a mothers' curse
that is
like no other
DAMN
all who
would hurt you.
I can
with a mothers' curse
that is like no other
DAMN
all who
would take your dreams
your hopes
and sully them
betray them

I can
with a mothers' love
that is like no other
give you
the sum
of my pain
the sum
of my joy
in being
WOMAN
and wish you . . . .
LOVE.

Freedom Child — Tilla's lullaby

And as I rock you
gently
I will sing.
I will sing to you
of skies dawning
to the bright lights —
of hope.
I will lull
I will lull
your slumber
not to the hollow
sounding thuds
of lash
on raw black flesh,
not to the clank
of chains,
but to a roar
from throats
Sounding freedom.
Sound freedom
into the ears
of generations,
pile edifices
to deeper freedom
truer freedom.

Sound freedom
won by Ogun's
reddened machetes
sound freedom
won in open war
in subterfuge.

And I will soothe
I will soothe
your sleep
with tales
of Toussaint, Dessalines
Cuffy, Cudjoe
Nanny and Boukman

I will show you
your ancestors
labelled warrior
and not victim.
I will teach you
a history of resistance.
Suck from my breasts
the will
to fight
the strength to
hope.
Suck from my breasts
my love.
It is a season
to bind
in
love

It is a
season
to sow seed
plant fruit
spawn fruit
spawn nations
I will sing . . . .
sing to you of
freedom

K*a*l*e*i*d*o*s*c*o*p*e

For Ursula Raymond

In fevered rush
to share
I thrust
with force
a flood of words
at closed
unwilling minds;
with joy
watch them yield
slowly —
hesitantly —
then with
warm rush
of response
sweetened by
unaccustomed pleasures
come back
for more
and more.
Insatiable now
unfullfilled now
by offerings
serving
but to
tease.
Awesome power
gives shape
to minds;
staunches
thirst
with words

that baulk
the parched winds
of ignorance.

Fearsome — the weight
to serve —
parallel
the moving machine's
might
by centred heritage
give my people light —
ignite
sparks
for imaginings;
stab
with conscious kaleidoscope
all darkness.

Images
For Earl Lovelace

Talons claw
a propanganda
path
spews poison
packaged
North.

Eagle filth
transposes
into print,
spreads
ennumbs
the mind.

Self retreats
from eagle beak
poised to
pluck out
destabilise
all eyes
seeing
filth
beneath the
gilt.

Eagle eyes
peer
into fallow
fecund fields,
loose earth
shaken free
from dugout

roots
ripe for
implantation.

Plant the gun
night in
night out.
Let sex
sell the products
sell the sisters short
in vacant plots
being filled
with poisoned garbage
packaged
North.

Numbered
lettered
Sesame seeds
sow
selfishness
grouchiness
amidst the
cartooned
violence.

The eagle
glances
backward,
Starved
naked talent
stalks his
gilded path
armed
only with self images
surviving still
in
secret enclaves —

SURE
he can bring
the eagle
DOWN.

For Astor
London '86

The drum is silent.
A wraith stands poised

The leaping spirit
cannot
be entombed
not yet
not yet

The wraith
spins lightly
into flight
from the cacaphony

The whirling mass
of black tormented flesh
dancing
to confused rhythms
the dance

of spiritual alientation

The death winds
of apathy
blow cold air
sweeping twirling
along the blaz-ed path
twining
through the centuries

The drum is silent
Feet twirl daintily

high step
pretty
blotting out
the fevered rhythms

The sound recedes —
cascading only
to feet pounding
in orchestrated rhythm
stage managed
well rehearsed
for politics and party.

Leave them!
Smiles the wraith;
poised in flight
leave them Eintou —
the time will come
perhaps the time
is not yet come

Drum sounds
fill the night
with sounds
of moaning;
of
whirling and stomping feet
and outstretched hands
of dancers
feeling pain;
of dancers
losing a strong
but gentle light

Invocations rise through
incense smoke.
The whirling is frantic
the drum pounds
the smoke billows

forming the wraith
passing
beyond
into the light
of eternity
glowing for
posterity.
A star shines
pointing the way
for a job
still to
be done,
But
for now,
the drum

falls silent.

Oil Spill

The oil spills
from the belly
of my mother
mixed with my blood
mixed with my sweat
tatooed across my history
in
struggle slogans.

The spilled oil
mixed with my blood
mixed with my sweat
burns in the crucible
and
in the unrelenting fires
of exploitation
turns to gold
for exportation
leaving
a
stench filled trail
I dead fish.
Butler's groans
join the ululation
of the dispossessed
undead
now paying the price
of unlearned lessons
of history.

The spill
becomes a trickle

the monkey on my back
packs
makes tracks
moves to easier
tracks
of exploitation.
Receding
leaves recession;
receding
leaves confusion;
paves a path
to turmoil
blood shed.

The monkey grins
picks its teeth,
burps loudly
belching
from
entrails
bloated
with oil
blood and sweat
and barling
and baring
its blooded fangs
vomits back
into a hungry basin
tiny globulins
of blood
oil
sweat
syncretized now
to aid.

The monkey howls
in glee
dances
round the basin

in obscence expectation
as hungry yard fowls
crowd to eat
and pay the price
of unlearned lessons
of history.

Blood Guilt For Maurice

I have no more tears
Those ducts have been
put through a wringer
of pain.
My soul has bled for
Walter
Mikey Smith
for Beverly
for Basil Davis
for Guy
and many more.
Now for Maurice
for Jackie

My generation bleeds
giving blood in hope
of giving life —
I have no more tears.

As mother
I feel my womb twist
in pain
for those who mourn
sons, daughters.

As woman
I feel the aching in my
guts
for those who lose
husbands, lovers.

As child
I feel the fearful void

of parents gone
to green the earth
they loved.

I have no more tears;
but still they come
wrung out from my
entrails
leaving the pain filled
guts dry, flaccid
still seeking to find
the courage
to go on
through mists of tears
that will not be denied.

My generation bleeds.
The bravest, strongest
spill their blood
in hope.
And powers large
loom to fight
battles of ideology
in Carib lands.
And powers large
loom to push
alien concepts
in our midst
belying
oft encanted myths
of sovereignty.

I watch my generation
bleed
I cry inside
Maurice, Maurice,
Maurice.
I have no more tears
but still they come unbidden.
History recycled.
Danton, Robespierre

Bolsheviks, Meneliks
L'Ouverture, Christophe.

Black blood shed
in vain pursuit
of alien ideologies
All armed
to re-enslave.

Power too,
dons the masks of ideology
in search of power
we turn into our own
entrails —
eat our own flesh
drink our own blood
from ritual calabashes
Grind our own bones
to dust
and feel lifted to new
heights of power.

The love power fades —
neglected.
The love power fades
rejected now
as weakness.
The God power stays
unused, unsolicited,
and frightened people
face the final
holocaust
fearing even
to cling together
in love
that alone
can save us.

I have not more tears
still
I have cause
to weep.

Capital C

I hear a cowboy
whoop with glee
pull the lasso tight
round cattle
strangled by his might.

Bomb them now —
no longer sheltered
by a crowned embrace.
Bomb them now
leaderless
totally displaced.
Bomb them now —
let them learn
to keep their place

I see a Capital C
running through my history.
I see a Capital C
kill Allende in
Chile.
Trample through this region
thirty times and three
already
in this century

Bomb them now
spreading wings in
Nicaragua.
Bomb them now
we coming for Cuba.
Bomb them now

and they'll learn
to keep their place.

I see some yardfowls
eating
from basins full of shame.
I see them taking money
to play the cowboy's game.
I see a people brainwashed
not to see the eagle
ripping through our guts.

Bomb them now
blood and destruction.
Bomb them now
call that liberation.
Bomb them now
let nought remain
of the revolution.
Bomb them now
they bound to learn
to keep their place.

I hear the boots come tramping
tramping from the right.
I see much blood being shedded
shedded from the right.
Yet I see my people looking
looking to the left
seeing through their blinders
the imaginary threats.

Bomb them now
revive McCarthy.
Bomb them now
in the name of democracy.
Bomb them now
they must learn
to keep their place.

I see my country fighting
for dignity and pride.
I see the yardfowls planning
to pick out we eye.
I see a Capital C
written in fire in the sky.

Bomb them now
they too uppitty.
Bomb them now
to disagree with me.
Bomb them now
bring dem to dey knee.
Bomb them now
let them learn
to keep their place.

I see a Capital C
written in fire in the skies.
I see a Capital C
followed by an I
blowing my legacy
to the skies
but I ent so easy
to destabilize.

Black Balled

Only
he
Who is without sin
Can bowl the ball
That will echo
on unmarked graves
of
Chaka
Dingaan
Ceteswayo.

* * * *

Only
he
Can dare be umpire
to say caught out
to those teamed to
men with blood
of
Xhosa
Zulu
Nguni
Ndebele
on their hands.

* * * *

Only
he
Who scores not himself so low
To see honour
In being substitute
for

white
Anglo
Saxon
Protestant.

* * * *

Only
he
who gets not stumped
by gilded balls
on field or off field
at
Uni lever
on board of Barclays
C.I.B.C. and even
West Indies Cricket Board of control
* * * *

Only
he
who refuses to bowl
his eager balls
in fair
moist fields
as climax pay for
playing
in
Bantuland

* * * *

Long leg of history
in the slips of time
spin off breaks
and take wickets of
men who play
at
politics
and think

its
cricket.

* * * *

And mountings of fast
furious attacks
come from those
who would bowl
bouncers at
their own
deny them smooth
deliveries
Of food, clothing,
shelter,
take money
not from playing
at the ball
of shame
but from the public purse.

* * * *

Thundering drums of naked feet
Of hordes of ghostly impi
In pilgrimage
From Blood River
To Sharpeville
To Soweto
Hold high their
bloodied shields
To block the balls
Of treachery.

* * * *

Only
he
Who is
without sin
Can bowl
the first ball.

The Underground
London '83

Faceless hooves
thunder through
cold corridors
of time.
Rythmic cacaphony
for nightmares
of Hitler's booted
army
of Reagan's booted
army
of Thatcher's booted
army
of Breznev's booted army
coming — coming —
at my brain
my heart
my soul;
hurrying hooves
urgently going
nowhere
every where
faceless hooves of
my own kind,
exiled kind
improving themselves
kind
confused kind
fighting back
kind
coming — coming —
at my mind
my heart

I want to go home.

White Rasta
London '83

I don't need nobody
to take my troubles to
cause I got Jah Jah
I got Jah Jah.

Mam, Brixton Market is my home
here where the music
plays,
with all these people milling
round,
that's how I spend my days.

'Cause
I don't need nobody
to take my troubles to,
cause I got Jah Jah
I got Jah Jah.

There's no music like black music,
the people are nice too;
that's why I spend my time
with them
the best thing I can do.

'Cause
I don't need nobody
to take my troubles to,
cause I got Jah Jah
I got Jah Jah.

Oh my people have gone crazy
on war, sex and money,
civilized to barbarity
nothing to offer me.

but
I don't need nobody
to take my troubles to,
cause I got Jah Jah
I got Jah Jah.

Look at my locks, do you like them?
They're not as nice as yours.
I'm just saying I'm
not one of those,
giving you all
the horrors.

and
I don't need nobody,
to take my troubles to
cause I got Jah Jah
I got Jah Jah.

This country blowing
my mind too,
and I belong right here
I can just imagine
what it doing to you.

but
I don't need nobody
to take my troubles to
cause I got Jah Jah
I got Jah Jah

Come hold my hand please sister.
We have to fight together
or else we'll never settle down
to live in unity.

Then we won't need nobody
to take our troubles to
cause we'll have Jah Jah
we'll have Jah Jah.

Jah Say

The sword of the Lord
will taste of our blood
When we yield
to the sins of the flesh!
For the rules from on high
should not be broken
by those knowing
better than the rest.
Jah Jah is God
Jah Jah's more than melody.

* * * *

The price of flouting
The rules of the Lord
is being beaten
With many stripes
and the scimitar
Will eat out our flesh
in many avenging stripes.
Jah Jah is God
Jah Jah's more than melody.

* * * *

For Jah Jah is a jealous God
he will not be mocked with song
For Jah Jah is God all seeing
beyond those flowing locks.
Jah Jah is God
Jah Jah's more than melody.

* * * *

Is a hard straight road we walking
and the Master's patience we wearing —
Brethren.
Jah Jah is God
Jah Jah's more than melody.

those bathing in Babylon's river
will not see Jah Jah's heaven
We gaining the whole world
and losing we soul —
The Lord's words we keep forgetting.
Jah Jah is God
Jah Jah's more than melody.

* * * *

What we giving the children as example?
We wallowing in crime and vice
Singing, chanting, talking 'bout Jah
and living between we with strife.
Jah Jah is God
Jah Jah's more than melody.

* * * *

Sisters you abusing
liquor you drinking
drugs destroying your brain,
shaming we people
keeping weself
From the prize of Jah Jah's heaven
Jah Jah is God
Jah Jah's more than melody.

* * * *

The sisters abusing Jah's holy temple,
the body he give us to cherish
We apeing Babylon

The values the standards
with the brothers we too will perish.
Jah Jah is God
Jah Jah's more than melody.

* * * *

Jah Jah say —
the brightness there to claim;
Jah Jah say
Doh only call me name,
Doh only sing me fame,
I stay more than de heavy sounds —
I stay more than de flowing robes —
I stay more than tossing locks —
I stay powerful and jealous God
waiting to guide mih flock.

* * * *

Jah Jah say
you tie up in gallery.
Jah Jah say
is pappyshow and mockery
Jah Jah say
The truth you not living
externals symbols you glorying
while you insides rottening
Jah Jah say
straighten out brethren
Before it too late
For the day of reckoning surely coming

Masquerade
For Peter Minshall

The River flows
full of
alien debris
flooding out
the fearful
picoplat
perched high
to flee
the flood
but not
escaping
laglee
spread on
errant
branches.

The River
flows
reddened
by
gallons of
Old Parr
that
try
in drunken
gulps
to stem
recession
tide.

The River
flows
drowning

washerwoman
mother
sister
daughter
in
tide
of
uncaring
male
dominance.

The River
vomits
up
swollen
dregs
of
drown-ded
humanity
no longer
able
to clutch
at
straws
of
survival.

The mas is
over
but
the masquerade
continues,
drowning
murmuring
streams
of
discontent
in
draughts

of
seeming
nonchalance.

The River
spawns
new
clawing
creeping
polluted
tentacles
of
destruction.

Flows
slow
sluggish
heavy
with
filth
corruption.
Leaving
trails
of
stench
filled mire.

The River
flows
swiftly
to
Armageddon —
saturated
now,
needing
cleansing
that
seems

to
beckon
rivers
of
blood.
And the fish
die
in the Gulf.

Cocksure

John cock fly high over
      the coop
   and laugh.
He flap he wing in
      de sun
   and laugh;
and he belly was heavy
      wid corn
and he beak was red
      wid blood.

Cok-y-oko
I Johnny could crow
cok-y-oko
I win dem and go
   cok-y-oko
Dey can't carre wid me
cause I is de king
   cock fighter Johnny.

I get de best training
   to be fighter to fear
   in a championships
   dey does have
   once in a five year.

Cok-y-oko
I Johnny could crow
cok-y-oko
I win dem and go
   cok-y-oko

Dey can't carre wid me
cause I is de king
cock fighter Johnny.

I build nest in east
I build nest in south
to tell you de truth
I build nest all about
cause cock dat fighting
serious like me
could always lan
in stew or curry.
Not me

Cok-y-oko
I Johnny could crow
cok-y-oko
I win dem and go
cok-y-oko
Dey can't carre wid me
cause I is de king
cock fighter Johnny.

Once a clean neck cock
that old name Sello
square up for me
and try to pelt blow
but I did hear
better cock dan he
crow

Cok-y-oko
I Johnny could crow
cok-y-oko
I win dem and go
cok-y-oko
Dey can't carre wid me
cause I is de king
cock fighter Johnny.

Watch de miles
  ah does cover
  an' you will discover
    dat
  I is a flyer
  of the highest order.
When I move on
  dey doh recover
Cause I is a lover
  like no odder.

Cok-y-oko
I Johnny could crow
cok-y-oko
I win dem and go
  cok-y-oko
Dey can't carre wid me
cause I is de king
  cock fighter Johnny.

Mih influence dread
  over living an dead
I have plenty big men
  quaking like hell
Dey getting real horrors
  from the tales ah could tell.

Cok-y-oko
I Johnny could crow
cok-y-oko
I win dem and go
  cok-y-oko
De can't carre wid me
cause I is de king
  cock fighter Johnny.

I eh so stupid
to get ketch in de ring
You know I from de lan

whey smart man is king
is to quit while you winning
and de opposition calkitaeing
cause I know that blood
go soon start running.

Cok-y-oko
I Johnny could crow
cok-y-oko
I win dem and go
cok-y-oko
Dey can't carre wid me
cause I is de king

cock fighter Johnny.

Woman as Artiste I
The Leap

The unexplored depths
in woman
scream for exposure.
The talent
submerged in service
stifles, atrophies
become vestigial.
Sometimes it survives
sublimated
unrecognised
untended.
Then recognition dawns,
precursor
of conflict,
frustration,
re-appraisal of self
re-deployment of energies,
re-arrangement of priorities.

How much energy for self
exploitation
of God given talent.
Is she not meant
to devote self
in service
to those her womb has spawned
and he
with whom she mates.
Guilt ridden
tormented
art demands her
as do her routines

She is pulled
hither and tither
making a mess of both
achieving disequilibrium
she recants
abjuring a doctrine
alien to upbringing.

Exploiting self!
That is heresy.
The smouldering fires
hide
in the deep recesses
of her being
nurtured
in masochistic isolation
she yearns
and yearns.
She misses the headiness
the soul searing release
of creative energies
successfully climaxed.

Once tasted
the want consumes.
And so,
some daring few
propelled by energies
that will not be
submerged
brave the gods
of servitude
of domesticity
unalloyed.

Letting the thread of art
weave a fabric of unity
between banal and blissful
twin facets of their being
are fused

they say
I am woman!
I must explore
my total self.

Woman As Artiste II: Spaced

The ladder
builds,
step, on step,
in uneven serration
wobbling
precariously upwards —
to dazzling heights
that will not stop
till stair and dream
confluence
in dizzying soarings
to
dazzling luminesences.
on sun bathed clouds.

The draughts of air
gulped now
fill my chest
painful
from breathing
laboured in upward toil.
Every rung
of painful ladder
climbed
gives air
burning the nostrils
forcing a pause
to grow accustomed
to the higher level

and air
more clear
more pure.

I know the fear
of stepping
into space,
or making a step
that's wrong
being pushed down
pulled down
slipping down
I dare not
look down.

Clouds beckon.
I shed a weight
of things
of people;
more things
most people
I do not
want
to climb
anymore,
there is nothing
no one
there
only pure air.
Clouds billow there
fragile
elusive
fugitive
as are dreams.

It is too much
to dare
to be so alone
and puny

in this heady
vastness.
I rest
looking down,
The crowded abyss
swims
in
dizzying eddying
invitation
to drop down
into the mass
of mess.
I'm so tired.

The murky water
beckons —
many hands stretch
in warm welcome
eyes look up
in jaundiced stares,
mouths say the words
I love
to hear —
used to!
used to!
my foot its down
one rung
and two —
stop the slipping
keep on climbing.

The wind is howling
in my ears
enveloping my brains
screaming for rest.
I feel the ache of
muscles
in agony
always now
in tension.

Soon,
the rains will come
in gentle showers,
and I will
close my eyes,
hold my face
to the sky
put my tongue out
to taste
the clean sharp taste —
let the tension drop
from limbs
that ache —
and rest
awhile;
and rest
awhile.

Woman As Artiste III: The Workplace

I went to work today
and stifled
struggled to breathe
in heavy undergrowth
of
non productivity.

I went to work today
saw
overseers enslaved
to beaurocracy
come late
feign
productivity.

Minds beggared
of ideas
marry fulfillment
to routine
mimicry
play plantation
games of
sterility

I went to work today
saw
jostling for promotion
games
pussy power
games
I'm a bigger shot than you
betty goatey
games

Try some obeah —
asafoetida and incense games
make them sick to dead
life and death
games
The Peter Principle obtains
for minds
beggared
of ideas.

Plantation unproductive
lapses
to jungle
slaves
wield whips
on slaves
grown
surly
seeking self — only.

I went to work today
saw slaves
rejecting
overseers
on corruption
on
piece of the
action.

Creativity
gasps,
struggles
to
infuse
new air
into the stench
of primal
jungle sweatings

Creativity
fears
foliated
tentacles,
dodges
weaves
barely atop
the carpet cushioned
jungle —
in
poised
dilemma
to flee
the putrid air
or
stay
at risk
of
dying.

One day
I will not
go to work.

Woman As Artiste IV: On Walking in the Rain To A London Bus Stop

Correct fare please
keep your ticket
you may need it

The mind strains
in desperation
to keep abreast
of eyes
roving in newness.
The feet
encumbered by the cold
struggle
beneath the weight
of unaccustomed clothes
clossetting
still icy fingers
still icy toes.
Here, there is no time
for futile tears
it's always to be doing
going
The urge to wonder
quickly flounders
in the face
of stark reality
and love
for my country
that loves not
its own soul.

Correct fare please
keep your ticket
you may need it

In envious rage,
grudging respect
There is encounter
with museums, libraries, theatres
hallowed monuments
to former
and the present great.
The mind turns inwards
homewards
to all the unnamed
panmen
of the hills
and others too —
neglected griots
of the tribe
never —
to be sculptured, reposed
forever —
in bronze, in stone
anyhow —
somehow —
in fitting epitaph.
Woe to my country
that loves not
its own soul

Correct fare please
keep your ticket
you may need it

The rain beats down
in gentle patter
persistent
like the ache for home
It is not the passion

not the fury
of tropic rain —
but dogged
unrelenting
as the hunched shoulders
slogging on
beneath it.
Watch the pavements.
If you kiss them
there'll be no hands
to help you up
and on the way,
keep your eyes
on the present
shelve the memories
of a country
that loves not its
own soul.

Correct fare please
keep your ticket
you may need it

Unrelenting haze
unabating showers
dim
cool
the pangs of torrid passions
from a different clime
a different time
Passions for people
for causes
unquenched by pressure
of reason there —
may dissipate —
here;
may self destruct
to reconstruct
a self —
aborted

by passions
for people
for causes
and a country
that loves not its
own soul.

Correct fare Please
keep your ticket
you may need it

Causes here
make time servers
of the brethren
holding tight
to pieces of the pie
dropping
into bleeding streets.
The wolves bay
in the bleeding streets
under the haze —
under the rain —
under the bared fangs
of survival
of exploitation.
Here, as there,
walk the few faithful
faceless, colourless,
tears misting, mixing
into the haze
the rain
persistent, pervading
like the love
for a country
that loves not its
own soul

The cold finds
crevices.
Every crack

admits the draughts
of unrequited love.
Wintry breezes
numb to harsh
reality.
The now is but to exhaust
all possibilty,
leave no regrets
moving past maturity
into eternity.
The star shines
through the haze
into eternity.
There are some
who cannot stay away —
from their country,
though it loves not
its own soul.

Correct fare please
keep your ticket
you may need it.

Out of the Shadows

Out of the shadows
leaping
into the light
of self knowledge.
Out of the shadows
into sharp focus.
Out of the shadows —
out of the shape
and images
pre-ordained
super-imposed;
moving now into
clear vision —
a mission
even —
for self
fulfilment.

Out of the shadows
into focus —
clear visibility
image no longer
shrouded
in shadow
of he
behind whom
it is said
I should walk.

Out of the shadows
out of oblivion

demanding
clear
compensation,
clear
recognition,
of roles
of functions.

Out of shadows
spitting
in the eye
of those who want me
still as burden bearer
of the race —
spitting in the eye
of those who say
only
helper supporter
screaming chanting
I come.

Out of shadows
into sharp focus
standing alone
nowhere
to lean
to rest,

Once — long ago.
I leaned
on the man
who walked
beside me
his knees wobbled
and I
balanced us both.
Balanced, he quickly
moved

from my side
leaving me
screaming

Out of the shadows
now
I come
screaming chanting
no longer despair
but
personhood
bare humanity
saying
it is time
I share
this burden.

At even time,
head bowed
feed shuffling
back aching
I have walked,
for centuries
from fields
of labour
to beds
of labour

Still — everywhere
the sun goes down
upon my shame;
my double curse
black — and
woman —
scraping the
barrel
of humanity,
wallowing

in my shame
my chains
wound tightly
over my mind
receiving
savage kicks
propelled by agony
by anguish
from a buised
bleeding castration
a running sore
for centuries
I come now
out of the shadows.
Of inarticulate
beast
of burden
weary
of taking strain
on my back
in my belly
knowing now
to take the kicks
is not
to heal
the wound
of centuries.

Out of the shadows
I stand
focussed
strong and knarled
like rock
buffetted by centuries
of harsh wind
and rough weather.

Out of the shadows
standing alone

nowhere to lean.
No longer
though
are the screams
those of despair,
of fear.
Defiant now
in sunlight
I walk
chanting personhood.

I balance myself
against the buffets
of harsh winds
and send out
a word
to sistren
groping still
to find a way
in the darkness
of
self
negation —
seeking
seeking
a way
out
seeking
seeking
simply
PERSONHOOD.